OF COURSE I CAN DO IT ALL
- I'M A MUM!

Mum's Contacts

Keeping connected

MUM IS ALWAYS RIGHT

(even when she is wrong!)

My important contacts

Name: ....

Number: ....

Name: ....

Number: ....

Name: ....

Number: ....

Name: ....

Number: ....

My Favourite Babysitters

Name: ....

GOOD FOR:

    MORNINGS   AFTERNOONS   EVENINGS

    ☐   ☐   ☐

Contact number: ....

....

Name: ....

GOOD FOR:

    MORNINGS   AFTERNOONS   EVENINGS

    ☐   ☐   ☐

Contact number: ....

....

Name: ....

GOOD FOR:

    MORNINGS   AFTERNOONS   EVENINGS

    ☐   ☐   ☐

Contact number: ....

....

Name: ....

GOOD FOR:

    MORNINGS   AFTERNOONS   EVENINGS

    ☐   ☐   ☐

Contact number: ....

....

Name: ....

GOOD FOR:

    MORNINGS   AFTERNOONS   EVENINGS

    ☐   ☐   ☐

Contact number: ....

....

Name: ....

GOOD FOR:

    MORNINGS   AFTERNOONS   EVENINGS

    ☐   ☐   ☐

Contact number: ....

....

Name: ....

GOOD FOR:

MORNINGS AFTERNOONS EVENINGS

☐ ☐ ☐

Contact number: ....

....

Name: ....

GOOD FOR:

MORNINGS AFTERNOONS EVENINGS

☐ ☐ ☐

Contact number: ....

....

Name: ....

GOOD FOR:

MORNINGS AFTERNOONS EVENINGS

☐ ☐ ☐

Contact number: ....

....

Name: ....

GOOD FOR:

MORNINGS AFTERNOONS EVENINGS

☐ ☐ ☐

Contact number: ....

....

Name: ....

GOOD FOR:

MORNINGS AFTERNOONS EVENINGS

☐ ☐ ☐

Contact number: ....

....

Name: ....

GOOD FOR:

MORNINGS AFTERNOONS EVENINGS

☐ ☐ ☐

Contact number: ....

....

NIGHT OUT!

School
Contacts

Teacher: ....

Phone/Email: ....

School: ....

Teacher: ....

Phone/Email: ....

School: ....

Teacher: ....

Phone/Email: ....

School: ....

Teacher: ....

Phone/Email: ....

School: ....

Teacher: ....

Phone/Email: ....

School: ....

Teacher: ....

Phone/Email: ....

School: ....

Teacher: ....

Phone/Email: ....

School: ....

Teacher: ....

Phone/Email: ....

School: ....

School Contacts

Teacher: .... Teacher: ....

Phone/Email: .... Phone/Email: ....

School: .... School: ....

Teacher: .... Teacher: ....

Phone/Email: .... Phone/Email: ....

School: .... School: ....

Teacher: .... Teacher: ....

Phone/Email: .... Phone/Email: ....

School: .... School: ....

Teacher: .... Teacher: ....

Phone/Email: .... Phone/Email: ....

School: .... School: ....

Teacher: ....

Phone/Email: ....

School: ....

'IF YOU CAN DREAM IT,
YOU CAN DO IT!'
Walt Disney

Teacher: ....

Phone/Email: ....

School: ....

Teacher: ....

Phone/Email: ....

School: ....

Teacher: ....

Phone/Email: ....

School: ....

Teacher: ....

Phone/Email: ....

School: ....

Teacher: ....

Phone/Email: ....

School: ....

Teacher: ....

Phone/Email: ....

School: ....

Teacher: ....

Phone/Email: ....

School: ....

PLAY
date

Play Date
Contacts

Name: ....

Telephone: ....

Email: ....

Name: ....

Telephone: ....

Email: ....

Name: ....

Telephone: ....

Email: ....

Name: ....

Telephone: ....

Email: ....

Name: ....

Telephone: ....

Email: ....

Name: ....

Telephone: ....

Email: ....

Name: ....

Telephone: ....

Email: ....

Name: ....

Telephone: ....

Email: ....

Name: ....

Telephone: ....

Email: ....

Name: ....

Telephone: ....

Email: ....

Name: ....

Telephone: ....

Email: ....

Name: ....

Telephone: ....

Email: ....

Name: ....

Telephone: ....

Email: ....

Name: ....

Telephone: ....

Email: ....

Name: ....

Telephone: ....

Email: ....

Name: ....

Telephone: ....

Email: ....

Name: ....

Telephone: ....

Email: ....

LOVE MORE, WORRY LESS

Name: ....

Telephone: ....

Email: ....

Name: ....

Telephone: ....

Email: ....

Name: ....

Telephone: ....

Email: ....

Name: ....

Telephone: ....

Email: ....

Name: ....

Telephone: ....

Email: ....

Name: ....

Telephone: ....

Email: ....

Name: ....

Telephone: ....

Email: ....

Name: ....

Telephone: ....

Email: ....

Name: ....

Telephone: ....

Email: ....

Name: ....

Telephone: ....

Email: ....

Name: ....

Telephone: ....

Email: ....

Name: ....

Telephone: ....

Email: ....

Name: ....

Telephone: ....

Email: ....

Name: ....

Telephone: ....

Email: ....

Name: ....

Telephone: ....

Email: ....

Name: ....

Telephone: ....

Email: ....

Kids' Contacts

Name: .... Telephone: ....

Activity: .... Email: ....

Name: .... Telephone: ....

Activity: .... Email: ....

Name: .... Telephone: ....

Activity: .... Email: ....

Name: .... Telephone: ....

Activity: .... Email: ....

Name: .... Telephone: ....

Activity: .... Email: ....

Name: .... Telephone: ....

Activity: .... Email: ....

Name: .... Telephone: ....

Activity: .... Email: ....

Name: .... Telephone: ....

Activity: .... Email: ....

Name: .... Telephone: ....

Activity: .... Email: ....

Name: .... Telephone: ....

Activity: .... Email: ....

Name: .... Telephone: ....

Activity: .... Email: ....

Name: .... Telephone: ....

Activity: .... Email: ....

Kids' Contacts

Parents

Parent: ....

Child: ....

Contact: ....

Parent: ....

Child: ....

Contact: ....

Parent: ....

Child: ....

Contact: ....

Parent: ....

Child: ....

Contact: ....

Parent: ....

Child: ....

Contact: ....

Parent: ....

Child: ....

Contact: ....

Parent: ....

Child: ....

Contact: ....

Parent: ....

Child: ....

Contact: ....

Car share & lifts

Parent: ....

Child: ....

Contact: ....

Parent: ....

Child: ....

Contact: ....

Parent: ....

Child: ....

Contact: ....

Parent: ....

Child: ....

Contact: ....

Parent: ....

Child: ....

Contact: ....

Parent: ....

Child: ....

Contact: ....

Parent: ....

Child: ....

Contact: ....

Parent: ....

Child: ....

Contact: ....

After-school activities & clubs

Activity/club: ....

Contact name: .... Day: ....

Contact number: .... Time: ....

Activity/club: ....

Contact name: .... Day: ....

Contact number: .... Time: ....

Activity/club: ....

Contact name: .... Day: ....

Contact number: .... Time: ....

Activity/club: ....

Contact name: .... Day: ....

Contact number: .... Time: ....

Activity/club: ....

Contact name: .... Day: ....

Contact number: .... Time: ....

Activity/club: ....

Contact name: .... Day: ....

Contact number: .... Time: ....

Activity/club: ....

Contact name: .... Day: ....

Contact number: .... Time: ....

Activity/club: ....

Contact name: .... Day: ....

Contact number: .... Time: ....

Activity/club: ....

Contact name: .... Day: ....

Contact number: .... Time: ....

Activities & Clubs

Time flies, enjoy life!

Activity/club: ....

Contact name: .... Day: ....

Contact number: .... Time: ....

Activity/club: ....

Contact name: .... Day: ....

Contact number: .... Time: ....

Activity/club: ....

Contact name: .... Day: ....

Contact number: .... Time: ....

Activity/club: ....

Contact name: .... Day: ....

Contact number: .... Time: ....

Activity/club: ....

Contact name: .... Day: ....

Contact number: .... Time: ....

Activity/club: ....

Contact name: .... Day: ....

Contact number: .... Time: ....

Activity/club: ....

Contact name: .... Day: ....

Contact number: .... Time: ....

Activity/club: ....

Contact name: .... Day: ....

Contact number: .... Time: ....

Activity/club: ....

Contact name: .... Day: ....

Contact number: .... Time: ....

Useful Contacts

Useful Contacts

Gardener: ....

Plumber: ....

Handyman: ....

Broadband
provider: ....

....

....

Library: ....

Cinema: ....

....

Useful Contacts

Doctor: ....

Doctor: ....

Doctor: ....

Doctor: ....

Dentist: ....

Orthodontist: ....

Optician: ....

Pharmacist: ....

Veterinary Clinc: ....

Birthdays & Anniversaries

Birthdays & Anniversaries

January

1	2	3	4	5	6
7	8	9	10	11	12
13	14	15	16	17	18
19	20	21	22	23	24
25	26	27	28	29	30
31					

February

1	2	3	4	5	6
7	8	9	10	11	12
13	14	15	16	17	18
19	20	21	22	23	24
25	26	27	28	29	

Birthdays & Anniversaries

March

1	2	3	4	5	6
7	8	9	10	11	12
13	14	15	16	17	18
19	20	21	22	23	24
25	26	27	28	29	30
31					

April

1	2	3	4	5	6
7	8	9	10	11	12
13	14	15	16	17	18
19	20	21	22	23	24
25	26	27	28	29	30

May

1	2	3	4	5	6
7	8	9	10	11	12
13	14	15	16	17	18
19	20	21	22	23	24
25	26	27	28	29	30
31					

June

1	2	3	4	5	6
7	8	9	10	11	12
13	14	15	16	17	18
19	20	21	22	23	24
25	26	27	28	29	30

July

1	2	3	4	5	6
7	8	9	10	11	12
13	14	15	16	17	18
19	20	21	22	23	24
25	26	27	28	29	30
31					

August

1	2	3	4	5	6
7	8	9	10	11	12
13	14	15	16	17	18
19	20	21	22	23	24
25	26	27	28	29	30
31					

September

1	2	3	4	5	6
7	8	9	10	11	12
13	14	15	16	17	18
19	20	21	22	23	24
25	26	27	28	29	30

October

1	2	3	4	5	6
7	8	9	10	11	12
13	14	15	16	17	18
19	20	21	22	23	24
25	26	27	28	29	30
31					

November

1	2	3	4	5	6
7	8	9	10	11	12
13	14	15	16	17	18
19	20	21	22	23	24
25	26	27	28	29	30

December

1	2	3	4	5	6
7	8	9	10	11	12
13	14	15	16	17	18
19	20	21	22	23	24
25	26	27	28	29	30
31					

Gift ideas

Gift ideas

Name: ....
Occasion: ....
Date: ....
Gift idea: ....
....
....
....

Name: ....
Occasion: ....
Date: ....
Gift idea: ....
....
....
....

Name: ....
Occasion: ....
Date: ....
Gift idea: ....
....
....
....

Name: ....
Occasion: ....
Date: ....
Gift idea: ....
....
....
....

Gift ideas

Name: ....

Occasion: ....

Date: ....

Gift idea: ....

....

....

....

Name: ....

Occasion: ....

Date: ....

Gift idea: ....

....

....

....

Name: ....

Occasion: ....

Date: ....

Gift idea: ....

....

....

....

Name: ....

Occasion: ....

Date: ....

Gift idea: ....

....

....

....

Gift ideas

Name: ....

Occasion: ....

Date: ....

Gift idea:

....

....

....

Name: ....

Occasion: ....

Date: ....

Gift idea:

....

....

....

Name: ....

Occasion: ....

Date: ....

Gift idea:

....

....

....

Name: ....

Occasion: ....

Date: ....

Gift idea:

....

....

....

Gift ideas

Name: ....

Occasion: ....

Date: ....

Gift idea:

....

....

....

Name: ....

Occasion: ....

Date: ....

Gift idea:

....

....

....

Name: ....

Occasion: ....

Date: ....

Gift idea:

....

....

....

Name: ....

Occasion: ....

Date: ....

Gift idea:

....

....

....

Gift ideas

Name: ....

Occasion: ....

Date: ....

Gift idea:

....

....

....

Name: ....

Occasion: ....

Date: ....

Gift idea:

....

....

....

Name: ....

Occasion: ....

Date: ....

Gift idea:

....

....

....

Name: ....

Occasion: ....

Date: ....

Gift idea:

....

....

....

Name: ....

Occasion: ....

Date: ....

Gift idea:

....

....

....

Name: ....

Occasion: ....

Date: ....

Gift idea:

....

....

....

Name: ....

Occasion: ....

Date: ....

Gift idea:

....

....

....

Name: ....

Occasion: ....

Date: ....

Gift idea:

....

....

Party
Planner

Use these pages to plan the special day.
Whether you are having your party at home or planning to hire a venue, spending some time planning ahead will help the day run smoothly and help everyone to have a wonderful time.

Party Planner

Party For: ....

Date: .... **Time:** ....

Theme: ....

Invitations: ....

Partyware: ....

Decorations: ....

Party bags: ....

Party games: ....

Entertainment (Face painter, Magician, Bouncy castle) ....

Food: ....

Cake ☐   **Thank you notes** ☐

Also need:

Party For: ....

Planner

Date: ....   Time: ....

Theme: ....

Invitations: ....

Partyware: ....
....

Decorations: ....
....

Party bags: ....
....

Party games: ....
....

Entertainment (Face painter, Magician, Bouncy castle) ....
....

Food: ....
....
....

Cake ☐   Thank you notes ☐

Also need:

Party Planner

Party For: ....

Date: .... **Time:** ....

Theme: ....

Invitations: ....

Partyware: ....
....

Decorations: ....
....

Party bags: ....
....

Party games: ....
....

Entertainment (Face painter, Magician, Bouncy castle) ....
....

Food: ....
....
....

Cake ☐ **Thank you notes** ☐

Also need:

Party Planner

Party For: ....

Date: .... Time: ....

Theme: ....

Invitations: ....

Partyware: ....
....

Decorations: ....
....

Party bags: ....
....

Party games: ....
....

Entertainment (Face painter, Magician, Bouncy castle) ....
....

Food: ....
....
....

Cake ☐   Thank you notes ☐

Also need: .

Don't Forget:

Christmas
gifts

Christmas gifts

Name: ....

Gift ideas:

....

....

Name: ....

Gift ideas:

....

....

Name: ....

Gift ideas:

....

....

Name: ....

Gift ideas:

....

....

Name: ....

Gift ideas:

....

....

Name: ....

Gift ideas:

....

....

Name: ....

Gift ideas:

....

....

Name: ....

Gift ideas:

....

....

Name: ....

Gift ideas:

....

....

Name: ....

Gift ideas:

....

....

Name: ....

Gift ideas:

....

....

Name: ....

Gift ideas:

....

....

Name: ....

Gift ideas:

....

....

Name: ....

Gift ideas:

....

....

So much to buy...
so little time

Name: ....

Gift ideas:

....

....

Name: ....

Gift ideas:

....

....

Name: ....

Gift ideas:

....

....

Name: ....

Gift ideas:

....

....

Name: ....

Gift ideas:

....

....

Name: ....

Gift ideas:

....

....

Name: ....

Gift ideas:

....

....

Christmas gifts

Name: ....

Gift ideas:

....
....
....

Name: ....

Gift ideas:

....

....

Name: ....

Gift ideas:

....

....

Name: ....

Gift ideas:

....

....

Name: ....

Gift ideas:

....

....

Name: ....

Gift ideas:

....

....

Name: ....

Gift ideas:

....

....

Christmas Card List

Name:

....

....

....

....

....

....

....

....

....

....

....

....

....

....

....

....

Year:

....

....

....

....

....

....

....

....

....

....

....

....

....

....

....

....

Name:

....
....
....
....
....
....
....
....
....
....
....
....
....
....
....
....
....
....

Year:

....
....
....
....
....
....
....
....
....
....
....

Christmas Card List

Name:

:::

:::

:::

:::

:::

:::

:::

:::

:::

:::

:::

:::

:::

:::

:::

Year:

:::

:::

:::

:::

:::

:::

:::

:::

:::

:::

:::

:::

:::

:::

:::

Peace Joy
Love

Family days & Weekend trips

Family days

Must go to:

....

....

Must go to:

....

....

Would love to go to:

....

....

Would love to go to:

....

....

Would love to go to:

....

....

Would love to go to:

....

....

Weekend trips

Must go to:

....

....

Must go to:

....

....

Would love to go to:

....

....

Would love to go to:

....

....

Would love to go to:

....

....

Would love to go to:

....

....

Ideas for the school holidays: Day trips

You are never too old to splash in the puddles and dance in the rain!

Turn your dreams into wonderful memories.

Ideas for the school holidays:
Weekends/Minibreaks

Ideas for the school holidays:
Places to visit

We may not have it all together,
but together we have it all.

Beauty Basics

....
....
....
....
....
....
....
....
....
....
....
....
....
....
....

Beach Essentials

Packing List

First Aid

·····································   ·····································
·····································   ·····································
·····································   ·····································
·····································   ·····································
·····································   ·····································
·····································   ·····································
·····································   ·····································
·····································   ·····································
·····································   ·····································
·····································   ·····································
·····································   ·····································
·····································   ·····································
·····································   ·····································
·····································   ·····································
·····································   ·····································

Don't forget

....
....
....
....
....
....
....
....
....
....
....
....
....
....
....
....
....

....
....
....
....
....
....
....
....
....
....
....
....
....
....
....
....

Back to
SCH

Back to school

Key dates for the new school year

....

....

....

....

....

....

....

....

....

....

....

....

....

*List here all the items you'll need,
so that you and your family are ready
for the new school year ahead.*

Meal Times

Have a delicious day!

Meals for the Week

What's for dinner tonight?

Monday: ....

Tuesday: ....

Wednesday: ....

Thursday: ....

Friday: ....

Saturday: ....

Sunday: ....

Monday: ....

Tuesday: ....

Wednesday: ....

Thursday: ....

Friday: ....

Saturday: ....

Sunday: ....

Monday: ....

Tuesday: ....

Wednesday: ....

Thursday: ....

Friday: ....

Saturday: ....

Sunday: ....

Monday: ....

Tuesday: ....

Wednesday: ....

Thursday: ....

Friday: ....

Saturday: ....

Sunday: ....

What's for dinner tonight?

Meals for the Week

Monday: ....

Tuesday: ....

Wednesday: ....

Thursday: ....

Friday: ....

Saturday: ....

Sunday: ....

Monday: ....

Tuesday: ....

Wednesday: ....

Thursday: ....

Friday: ....

Saturday: ....

Sunday: ....

Monday: ....

Tuesday: ....

Wednesday: ....

Thursday: ....

Friday: ....

Saturday: ....

Sunday: ....

Monday: ....

Tuesday: ....

Wednesday: ....

Thursday: ....

Friday: ....

Saturday: ....

Sunday: ....

My Favourite Recipes

Recipe: .... Serves: .....

Ingredients:
....
....
....
....
....
....

Method:
....
....
....
....
....
....
....
....
....

Recipe: .... Serves: .....

Ingredients:
....
....
....
....
....
....

Method:
....
....
....
....
....
....
....
....
....

Recipe: .... Serves: .....

Ingredients:
....
....
....
....
....

Method:
....
....
....
....
....
....
....
....
....

Recipe: .... Serves: .....

Ingredients:
....
....
....
....
....

Method:
....
....
....
....
....
....
....
....
....

Recipe: .... Serves: ......
Ingredients:
....
....
....
....

Method:
....
....
....
....
....
....
....

Recipe: .... Serves: ......
Ingredients:
....
....
....
....

Method:
....
....
....
....
....
....
....

Recipe: .... Serves: ......
Ingredients:
....
....
....
....

Method:
....
....
....
....
....
....
....
....

Recipe: .... Serves: ......
Ingredients:
....
....
....
....

Method:
....
....
....
....
....
....
....
....

My Favourite Recipes

Recipe: _____ Serves: _____
Ingredients:
_____
_____
_____
_____
_____

Method:
_____
_____
_____
_____
_____
_____
_____
_____
_____

Recipe: _____ Serves: _____
Ingredients:
_____
_____
_____
_____
_____

Method:
_____
_____
_____
_____
_____
_____
_____
_____
_____

Recipe: _____ Serves: _____
Ingredients:
_____
_____
_____
_____
_____

Method:
_____
_____
_____
_____
_____
_____
_____

Recipe: _____ Serves: _____
Ingredients:
_____
_____
_____
_____
_____

Method:
_____
_____
_____
_____
_____
_____
_____

Recipe: _____ Serves: ___
Ingredients:

Method:

Recipe: _____ Serves: ___
Ingredients:

Method:

Recipe: _____ Serves: ___
Ingredients:

Method:

Recipe: _____ Serves: ___
Ingredients:

Method:

Mum's time

Give yourself a break—seriously!

My precious time

Hairdresser Contact Name: ....
....
Number: ....

Hairdresser Contact Name: ....
....
Number: ....

Manicure Contact Name: ....
....
Number: ....

Manicure Contact Name: ....
....
Number: ....

Hair appointments

....

....

....

....

....

....

....

....

....

....

....

....

Nail appointments

....

....

....

....

....

....

....

....

....

....

....

....

My perfect treats

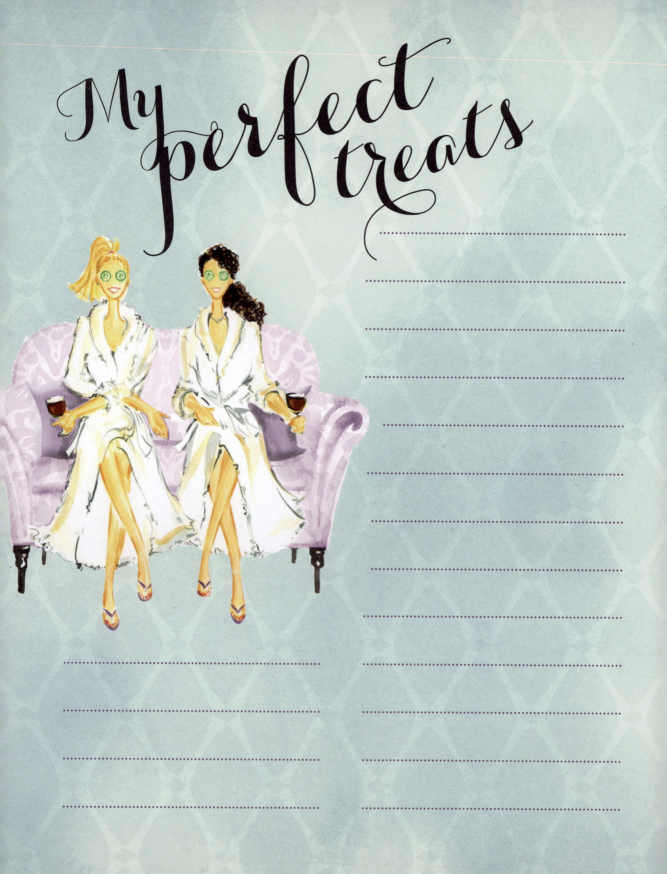

....

....

....

....

....

....

....

....

....

....

....

....

....

....

....

....

....

....

....

....

....

....

....

....

ENJOY TODAY, IT'S SPECIAL.

Plans for a

Girls' night out

....

....

....

....

....

....

....

....

Great friends never go out of fashion.

Mum's notes

WITH A FABULOUS PAIR OF HEELS,
ANYTHING IS POSSIBLE.

Mum's
notes

Mum's notes

Every day may not be good, but there is something good in every day.

Mum's notes

Mum's notes

When you stop and look around,
This life is pretty amazing.

....
....
....
....
....
....
....
....
....
....

Mum's notes

Mum's notes

Dream Big

Mum's notes

Mum's busy day

....

....

....

....

....

....

....

....

....

....

....

....

So much to do...

but first my coffee!

So much to do, but

....

....

....

....

....

....

....

....

first I need a hug!

To do

....
....
....
....
....
....
....
....
....
....
....
....
....

Mum's List

To do

....
....
....
....
....
....
....
....
....
....
....
....

Mum's List

To do

·····································
·····································
·····································
·····································
·····································
·····································
·····································
·····································
·····································
·····································
·····································
·····································
·····································
·····································
·····································

Mum's List

To do

·····································
·····································
·····································
·····································
·····································
·····································
·····································
·····································
·····································
·····································
·····································
·····································
·····································
·····································

Mum's List

To do today

·······································
·······································
·······································
·······································
·······································
·······································
·······································
·······································
·······································
·······································
·······································
·······································
·······································
·······································
·······································
·······································

Mum's List

To do today

·······································
·······································
·······································
·······································
·······································
·······································
·······································
·······································
·······································
·······································
·······································
·······································
·······································
·······································
·······································
·······································

Mum's List

To do today

·····································
·····································
·····································
·····································
·····································
·····································
·····································
·····································
·····································
·····································
·····································
·····································
·····································
·····································
·····································

Mum's List

To do today

·····································
·····································
·····································
·····································
·····································
·····································
·····································
·····································
·····································
·····································
·····································
·····································
·····································

Mum's List

To do today

....
....
....
....
....
....
....
....
....
....
....
....
....
....

Mum's List

To do today

....
....
....
....
....
....
....
....
....
....

Mum's List

To do today

....

....

....

....

....

....

....

....

....

....

....

....

....

....

....

Mum's List

To do today

....

....

....

....

....

....

....

....

....

....

....

....

Mum's List

Must do today

....
....
....
....
....
....
....
....
....
....
....
....
....
....

Mum's List

Must do today

....
....
....
....
....
....
....
....
....
....
....
....

Mum's List

Must do today

....
....
....
....
....
....
....
....
....
....
....
....
....
....
....

Mum's List

Must do today

....
....
....
....
....
....
....
....
....
....
....
....

Mum's List

To do after a cup of ....

....
....
....
....
....
....
....
....
....

Mum's List

To do after a cup of ....

....
....
....
....
....
....
....
....
....
....
....
....
....
....

Mum's List

To do after
a cup of ....

Mum's List

To do after
a cup of ....

Mum's List

It's a miracle if it all gets done list!

....

....

....

....

....

....

....

....

....

....

Mum's List

To do today

....

....

....

....

....

....

....

....

....

....

....

....

....

....

....

Mum's List

To do today

· ·
· ·
· ·
· ·
· ·
· ·
· ·
· ·
· ·
· ·
· ·
· ·

Mum's List

It's a miracle if it all gets done list!

· ·
· ·
· ·
· ·
· ·
· ·
· ·
· ·

Mum's List

Must do today

....
....
....
....
....
....
....
....
....
....
....
....
....
....
....

Mum's List

Must do today

....
....
....
....
....
....
....
....
....
....
....
....
....
....
....
....
....
....
....

Mum's List

Must do today

....
....
....
....
....
....
....
....
....
....
....
....
....
....
....
....
....
....

Mum's List

Must do today

....
....
....
....
....
....
....
....
....
....
....
....
....
....
....
....

Mum's List

The chic shopper's shopping list

....
....
....
....
....
....
....

Mum's List

The chic shopper's shopping list

....
....
....
....
....
....
....
....
....
....

Mum's List

The chic shopper's shopping list

....
....
....
....
....
....
....
....
....
....
....
....
....
....
....
....
....

Mum's List

The chic shopper's shopping list

....
....
....
....
....
....
....
....
....
....
....
....
....
....
....
....
....
....

Mum's List

My wish list for the next shopping trip

···
···
···
···
···
···
···
···
···
···
···
···

Mum's List

My wish list for the next shopping trip

···
···
···
···
···
···
···

Mum's List

My wish list for the next shopping trip

....
....
....
....
....
....
....
....
....
....
....
....
....
....
....
....

Mum's List

My wish list for the next shopping trip

....
....
....
....
....
....
....
....
....
....
....
....
....
....
....

Mum's List

Mum's shopping list

....
....
....
....
....
....
....
....
....
....
....
....
....

Mum's List

Mum's shopping list

....
....
....
....
....
....
....
....
....
....
....
....
....
....
....

Mum's List

Mum's shopping list

....
....
....
....
....
....
....
....
....
....
....
....
....
....
....
....

Mum's List

Mum's shopping list

....
....
....
....
....
....
....
....
....
....
....
....
....
....

Mum's List

Mum's shopping list

....
....
....
....
....
....
....
....
....
....
....
....
....
....
....

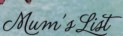

Mum's List

Mum's shopping list

....
....
....
....
....
....
....
....
....
....
....
....
....
....
....
....

Mum's List

Mum's shopping list

....
....
....
....
....
....
....
....
....
....
....

Mum's List

Mum's shopping list

....
....
....
....
....
....
....
....
....
....
....

Mum's List

Shopping Essentials

I must get ....

....

....

....

....

....

....

....

....

....

....

....

Mum's List

Shopping Essentials

I must get ....

....

....

....

....

....

....

....

....

....

....

....

....

....

Mum's List

Shopping Essentials

I must get ....

....

....

....

....

....

....

....

....

....

....

....

....

....

....

....

Mum's List

Shopping Essentials

I must get ....

....

....

....

....

....

....

....

....

....

....

....

....

....

....

....

....

Mum's List

My shopping list

I must get ....

....
....
....
....
....
....
....
....
....
....
....
....
....
....
....
....
....
....

Mum's List

My shopping list

I must get ....

....
....
....
....
....
....
....
....
....
....
....
....
....
....
....
....
....
....

Mum's List

My shopping list

I must get

....

....

....

....

....

....

....

....

....

....

....

....

....

....

....

....

....

Mum's List

My shopping list

I must get

....

....

....

....

....

....

....

....

....

....

....

....

....

....

....

....

....

Mum's List

Mum's shopping list

I must get ....
....
....
....
....
....
....
....
....
....
....
....
....
....
....
....

Mum's List

Mum's shopping list

I must get ....
....
....
....
....
....
....
....
....
....

Mum's List

Mum's shopping list

I must get

....

....

....

....

....

....

....

....

....

....

....

....

....

....

....

....

Mum's List

Mum's shopping list

I must get

....

....

....

....

....

....

....

....

....

....

....

....

Mum's List

My amazing grocery shopping list

....
....
....
....
....
....
....
....
....
....
....
....
....
....

Mum's List

My amazing grocery shopping list

....
....
....
....
....
....
....
....
....
....
....
....
....
....
....

Mum's List

My amazing grocery shopping list

....

....

....

....

....

....

....

....

....

....

....

....

....

....

....

....

....

....

....

....

Mum's List

My amazing grocery shopping list

....

....

....

....

....

....

....

....

....

....

....

....

....

....

....

....

....

....

Mum's List

My shopping list

······································
······································
······································
······································
······································
······································
······································
······································
······································
······································
······································
······································
······································
······································
······································

Mum's List

My shopping list

······································
······································
······································
······································
······································
······································
······································
······································
······································
······································
······································
······································
······································
······································
······································

Mum's List

My shopping list

....
....
....
....
....
....
....
....
....
....
....
....
....
....
....
....
....
....
....
....
....
....

Mum's List

My shopping list

....
....
....
....
....
....
....
....
....
....
....
....
....
....
....
....
....
....
....
....
....
....

Mum's List

My amazing grocery shopping list

....
....
....
....
....
....
....
....
....
....
....
....
....
....
....

Mum's List

My amazing grocery shopping list

....
....
....
....
....
....
....
....
....
....
....
....
....
....

Mum's List

My amazing grocery shopping list

....
....
....
....
....
....
....
....
....
....
....
....
....

Mum's List

My amazing grocery shopping list

....
....
....
....
....
....
....
....
....
....
....
....
....
....
....
....

Mum's List

....
....
....
....
....
....
....
....
....
....
....

The chic shopper's
To Do list .

....
....
....
....
....
....
....

....
....
....
....
....

Mum's List

Mum's List